WINGMAKERS

WINGMAKERS

POEMS BY
BRITNY CORDERA

WITH ART BY
DAVID H. L. BURTON

PINYON PUBLISHING
Montrose, Colorado

Cover & Interior Art Copyright © 2015 by David H. L. Burton

Photograph of Britny Cordera by Atiim Jones
Photograph of David H. L. Burton by himself

Design by Susan Elliott

First Edition: February 2015

Pinyon Publishing
23847 V66 Trail, Montrose, CO 81403
www.pinyon-publishing.com

Library of Congress Control Number: 2015930977
ISBN: 978-1-936671-29-8

Acknowledgments

I would like to acknowledge the following people and publications:

Silver Birch Press for featuring "Urania the Stargazer" in their *Mythic Poetry Series*; and Pinyon Publishing for publishing "Phoenix," "The Reborn," and "The Sensualist" in *Pinyon Review*.

My dear friend, D. J. Carlile, The Hierophant, for editing an early draft of *Wingmakers*; David for putting up with me and for the wonderful illustrations; patron to *Wingmakers* and local artist, Bart Vargas; Gary Entsminger and Susan Elliott for bringing *Wingmakers* to fruition; and my mom for supporting my passion and helping me reach my goals.

You hold my eternal gratitude, love, and respect.

To the Bard of Owls whose 3 AM song

gave birth to these poems

And to my own Euterpe

Never regret thy fall,
O Icarus of the fearless flight
For the greatest tragedy of them all
Is never to feel the burning light

—Oscar Wilde

CONTENTS

FAMILY THREE
SOUTHERN SKIES

POSTLUDES

URANIA THE STARGAZER

With dewish wand, I point
to the unborn words of wind-
driven ballerinas.
I knew their stories before
my star-dotted lyre gave flight
to the fledged songbirds and carrions.
I make sure time does not pluck
your crown and quill, but
you refuse my globe on palace walls.
My cut-out eyes find home
on fountains of blue-backs where
quince trees know no lore filled
more with woe.
I placed clap-nets where grottoes
roofed your flared arms,
no brighter than my wonder
for sky beyond blue.
You, the ones who fly, live now in space
where a hoot, tweet, caw, coo,
and broken trill, flood images of
swans who die for Elysium—
through small white frames, my
feathering fingers lure the tizzy
of wings to clear stage; empty curtain.
Now, fauns and flat-foots can voyage
alone, but hear your mummed whispers.
The common raven will make man marvel
for his yearning din.
Urania I'm named.
On my cloak, all runes you've cast.

PHANTOM HORACE

Feel the sky
of ocean tide
grace tropic-painted wings—

Watch the hands
of time sculpt
breath beneath marbled
bones, then to rip

your ruby wine
from flesh gone slack—

Smell, taste
the music sung
from silence hung
on gilded thorns

O how the bard
of rose-lipped phantoms
feels the inked stream
echo rippling history.

O how metaphor gnaws
through vast sweeps
of albicant, to bond
with feathers, sarcoline.

Forever eat ambiguity's
willingly offered flame.

BUTTERFLY'S NIGHTMARE

You
look
up at
sun's blue sky,
expecting to watch
cloud-pulled day, instead there she lies:
the mute moon. Wrinkles

on
the mossy
fish leave your
eyes to wonder, if
you'd forget the tune of your dust-
covered wings

while
frost
bitten
nostalgia
burns orange holes where you
dipped your head in crystal. The dew

should
have told
you to tend
your weak laurels,
but now your satin arms can not
carry you through salt-
less sky.

I
will
my kiss
to carry
you home high where the
silver night sliver cradles dreams
fossilized

Up-
on
ancient,
vanilla-
scented books, you learned
how fragile the sticks and stones
your mind's eye can see.

You
learned
that M-
shaped insects,
buzzing in the brain,
live two moons before they live on
as memories.

FAMILY ONE

NORTH CELESTIAL POLE

SINGE RED

Words weaved by bowing sun's thousand fingers
summon emotions trapped behind steel sky.

Pear trees with waltzing muse, beg full moon nymphs
for lulling mist to bear the dancing floor.

Flames of Solstice no longer raze stilled wings—
only autumn crocus wanders before

frost cradles my mother close to his breast.
Her time mummifies under blizzard quilts;

still tells tales of harvest crescent and stars.
Pan, sipping his rotten wine, lamps fall's wave

as white peafowl spreads his tail of Argus
eyes—stretching from the centuries' slumber.

He speaks the secret tongue of dreaming Sphinx
who dreams of frigid Draco's breath stripping

wooded maidens. Can you smell Russian sage
bleed blue for the poet's rain? No, not now.

Golden mane, steeped in the scent of singe red,
the sound of scared wind, the taste of bon fire

must find palaces in constellations
or torrid blank scrolls. Winter is not kind.

NOAH'S PIGEON OR ARGO'S DOVE

Waddle on the hunter's belt with me
while I tell you how I brought land
to sea and peace to the brawl
                    of rock islands

"Bird from Peace"
Ha! I fooled the siring symbols.
Like the competitive sister
                Clashing Rocks,
young ones
rely on the name squab
for our art of squabbling
                    to death.

Unlike rocks though,
they were once the poor man's dinner;
rice—their blankets of notoriety,
olives served on side.

And even though they still eat my
youth, what life is there without
those biped-monkeys? After they are gone,
who will master
            my morning coo-oo?

At least my tufts are of some use
to the winged diaper boy.
Red arrows tipped with white quill,
awaken the slumbering thumper.

Anyway, I never really found land;
                never really
                calmed the fight of boulders

only puked up the dirty branch
stuffed down my throat
night before last
on the wretched boat—
                Only fleeced
                        the golden fleece
                                before the faux hero.

THE WINDUP DRAGON

One head is not enough
to guard the golden apple tree
from nymphs who guard them too,
the meat head would not have found me.
To guard the golden apple tree
in the bowels of Cyrene,
the meat head would not have found me
if pack mule dropped his clod and cloud.
In the bowels of Cyrene
when my hundred heads ended,
pack mule dropped clod and cloud.
My minced teeth morphed the first five Thebans
when hundred heads ended,
I grew golden crest, poison-sated breath.
Minced teeth morphed the first five Thebans,
where three sharp prongs bit my tongue,
I grew golden crest, poison-sated breath.
Fire replaced my eyes,
where three sharp prongs hid my words.
I promise I've had better times
when fire became my eyes.
Ancients once kissed my four claws and twisting torso.
These were my better times
when they tickled my fins or stag horns.
Ancients once kissed my four claws and twisting torso,
but why do you think I am snake?
When you tickled my fins or stag horns,
I saw my body in the sky.
Why do you think I am snake?
Eighth biggest in the stars, but I am coiled.
You see my body in the sky,
by vestal poet's hands.
Eighth biggest in the stars, but coiled, I am.
I did not fight for my life
by vestal poet's hands.
Instead I wanted to freeze.
I did not fight for my life
and nymphs no longer guard trees.
I wanted the eternal frost: wound, I remained
warm. One head was never enough.

PARAKEET

Woman walking with rainbow-stained bird
in hand, tells the many stories
the chirper goes unheard.

Feathered flyer is the words
of her childhood and present worries.
Walking with rainbow-stained bird

her eyes are clear, not blurred
by the voice of echoing furies.
The chirper goes unheard.

Dresses of night try to slur
the bards flurry who
walks with rainbow-stained bird.

She then, with leafy light, chauffeured
the once mythed fury.
Chirper still goes unheard.

Grey hair is the world's word.
Pseudo parrot should speak harmoniously.
Walk with rainbow-strained bird,

The chirper that goes unheard.

IMMORTAL WINGS

I lie,
patiently resting in the chest
of the snake queen, for the time
to spread my wings.
But my fate is torn in two by
the Gorgon and the sea.

What an irresponsible fool
for defiling the once most beautiful creature.

Though, I wouldn't be
in the north sky
if not for you.
I sprang from my mothers
stony blood, proud and ready to fly.

I am called springs;
the rocky ways of purity, for I helped

my friends
forge lions from vulnerables
so the gods had toys to de-
mortalize. As I danced to their stories and songs,
I struck ground where the poet's

fountain gently flows.
Words are born from these waters.

Brave man, who killed fire-breathing
monsters, was the only one who tamed
me with wisdom's gilded bridle.
Otherwise you will see me

fly freer and higher than the
wind-dragged clouds.

The second
heroes head held too high, shattered.
He would not haunt me if
I caught him,

> but the invisible lights
> have heads higher than the stars.

Look at me! You will not turn to stone
my stare only speaks of glory.
Unlike my father, water is not
the love of my life.

> I only birth liquid on
> waterless mountains.

When I made it to the castle
in the sky, thunder boy made me
the eleventh biggest above the blue,
but where did he put my other half?

> My secret twin,
> he is the one called golden sword.

READING WOMAN

With head,
        like those of fledgeling birds—
shaped nose, features pinched—
Old and blue-grey reading woman
        shoves her head in the golden bath
of shapeless words.
Her reflection,
        so piercingly kin
with nature, does not shift
        her eyes from books
eating butterflies,
        she claims they cause
the burning memory.
While mauve shadows faintly tink
        and prick at the question;
"what reading woman reads,"
she does not hesitate to breathe
        the dusky air that belongs to
her palms.
Smooth, crooked cover, hovers
        above her. She pokes and prods
at the hidden veils
        iridescing the bright
black hole of alphabet.
Bowls filled
        with porcupine quills, elevate her hunger
to empty moons where
        empty metaphor drives reading woman
to carve her name
        in nameless boughs
of dialogue.

FAMILY TWO

GLORY OF HERCULES

THE NEBULA WALTZ

"Danse avec moi dans le ciel de nuit."
Taurus beckoned to Pisces
cold wind through the ears whispered
the flames that would become their dance floor.
Taurus, touch the glossy, wet fin
of the two-tailed fish.
Violet auras radiate from the sun
become blind by the starry fire.
Dance the dance
of orchids hanging
in the hanging gardens, they fly.
The horned one tastes the wine
of stars and sees the Herculean tale
shaded by blue leaves, little spider woman
sleeps at the feet of the bull and the fish.
Their icy toes flame her hearth.
Bridges form gateways
to the tree of truth for eyes alone to see.
The broken red string of fate
knows no boundary between beating cores.
White hairs
form mountains on bull's back.
Pisces calls this home.
Let the gardens hang from your breath.

TO APOLLO

Arid heavens ricochet a serpent's
promise beneath crooning cobalt soil
a tale of those birds he stalked
like the hill's black roar
to the idea
       of a dreaming sun.
But the sun does not dream
for he is stuck in the embrace
of a past stained
scribe's blood, carved
on the little maidens roots and heart-
                    wood.
He warms, with lanterns
birthed from sweating caves,
the lost hum of grape groves
only to scratch glass
skins of fruit whose fingers pine
       for his flailing crown—
Fruit who need a breath
from the crying branches
of breasted tree;
the lover that raised
and killed
       her seeds.
Threads of history will no
longer convey her old vines
to the ends
of fields where exalted tenants
repeat their glutted lives
             their glutted lives
        glutted lies

Like the snake
who flies through gardens
that walk on spruce stilts,
the sun falls
to knees when shadows
eat his laurel—
when ocean eats his
                    spinning chariot.

MUTE SWAN

Hair turned feather
       as long neck
        grew from breasts.

Fingers webbed
       as wings clothed
        nude arms.

Watching teeth fall from my mouth,
       orange muzzle
        fitted to lucid lips,

I mourned for the fallen sun children—
       the bard
        and the baby carriage.

Sable tears still fill my eyes
       become my
        noble mask.

You do not know I tremble faced
       with flame, wind,
        stone

gnawing at my nerves,
       the nightmares they bring
        you will never see

me fly while his father flares around,
       while blue
        skies hide

eagles and traitors.
        You will not see
        me pirouette with

ground who smothers breath
        when I coup
        my dread.

Water is nepenthe,
        my sorrow-
        less maiden.

As Earth slumbers, I live
        for Lyra he tore
        from my tree,

never to know which thread is true.
        I was once
        Cygnus.

THE SENSUALIST

No, I am not the raven who brings
    sickness and death to your front
        lawn as I scavenge for my next meal.

No, I am not the raven who fights
    for the head of the pink, pluck'd
        bird. With plumes of silver or rainbow

I never brought water
    for Jupiter's feast
        I am the gluttonous

deceiver; lover to the fig tree,
    yet in anger, he found
        my palace next to the fire ball I stole—

next to the waterless cup—
    next to the snake I blamed.
        I am sage

of tricksters,
    changing night to day and day to night.
        If you listen to my whispers

you may hear the gossip of time.
    I will never be starved
        like my rottenly friends.

Thirst is my curse
    Cursed mother of medicine; flame of the sun,
        you blackened my feathers wooing

destined corpse.
  Cawing veils
    my cunning, winged wisdom.

Little does he know, throwing
  pebbles in a pitcher makes water rise.
    Serpent in beak

forgave the charioteer,
  but I still remain
    sickly sacred symbol.

Let me remind you of your duality;
  healer and harbinger of plague
    while Peacock keeps my painted wings.

THUNDERBIRD

Nectar beast of burden
our own prince of cups
was not yet bearded
when talons
sealed his youth
in the call of a lightning bolt.
Only greed would bleed for
rooster's silent cry
frostily lingered from his tongue
through spine—
"O singing thunder, take me!"

Will you ever know
my two-faced hush?
We are both the boy hidden
in attic, bound to the sky
in hand,

cloud giant our statue once
when I flew men disguised
as talking cows off sandy
islands. Those who ate his eggs
drowned in baths of glass elephants

We swallow
your freedom
etched in casts of snakes
for I see no woods
between sex on your fingers
war painted on skull.
Fertile earth nests where winds
lick salty mountains.

I shot the dove-downed arrow,
booned dried storm cupids victim.
Now no nymph can hide
from sunlit eyes
while vulture warms our seedy fruit—

(Moon high, moon low,
he chases random
rotting granate seeds)
I wonder

are we the swan?
Or is Love the eagle?
I allowed myself to dominate me?

FOR THE MOON

Crows and cranes fly high while you ripen—
under shaded green clouds and little girls wear quartz
to speak with stars. When you hear owls and trees howl
pluck your earlobe and hair; feed it to the hungry wind
who grants you the wish to forgive
the frozen hands who desire mittens.

See, gray creatures that walk on stilts, wear mittens—
one foot, two paw, too. Worms in ripe
apples, now live on walls as they forgive
their mold home. O'er there, sane rain fills glass quartz
for your drinking pleasures on windless
twilight. Remember, no secret hides from the howl.

Dancing poppies and three-legged wolves hear the outhowl
of the cracked, wooded instrument. His master knows no mittens
on this arctic night as the snow-fraught wind
tears at the spine of the red ripened
violin. Old lady peers through rosy, clear quartz—
whispers to the leaves of the moon's forgiveness.

But how can the ones with wings forgive
winter for coming too soon? They howl
for their lives as they freeze in quartzy
icebergs. If only the one who made mittens
made a kind of glove for feathers, ripened
berries would freely fly with the wind.

Blue and red moons walk up and down winding
stairs like planets. They are most unforgiving
to the salty waters of the ripe
green seas who cradle dizzy howlets.
That does not move the smitten
fruits who have the power to see through quartz.

You, the bringer of stories, deserve a quart
of wine and nectar, but do not fly with the wind
that does not feel like mittening
your screams. I promise the trees forgave
the lotuses for their bloody, nightly howling.
Hold the hearts of Bird of Paradise, watch them ripen—

Before your quartz eyes see in night and forgive
the wind-taught howl.
Forget to wear mittens? Just let sun ripen forest seeds.

FAMILY THREE

SOUTHERN SKIES

TUMBLEWEED

When rain gives in
to misty plains—
when storms of tidal
heat bow to thundering polar
breeze—your virid, tender
fingers curl in frailless
clay bowls. Upon your runes,
unwritten, banished
by sand-laden sedge,
your darkling shell
unhinged from fire's garden.
Wind feeds your fate—
you cling to unclipped
wings and hurried feet
who claim home
to the many-faced moon,
for she knows
no winter—knows no
solitary among vocal stars.
You own no direction
among these tonal paths—
Life from death
new from old,
no legends hold your sovereign
song to mauve
dreams of crows.
As you roll, wandering root-
less palm, bring forth amaranth's
pride nestled in your bones.

THE REBORN

I rise from my ashes, I claim new life.
I bow to my flames; one more shadow
     devoured by time.
My future, wrought in past.
     It's not wrong to call me the morning star,
but I am not the center of your world.
     I am the avian of cycles just as my
scarlet, blue, purple, and gold
     crests are more or less radiant with
each rise and fall.
     Unlike the others with wings and feathers,
I do not live on fruit and flowers.
     Gumming incense and balsam sap
are all it takes to live 500 more years.
     Let my centennial death and rebirth
serve a nuance more than the rising and
     setting sun.
My eyes hold tenderness equal to Eagle's terror,
     so my beautiful song
rings though the ages and
     you may hear my cry.
I will no longer wander
     the water-starved abyss,
once I give symbols and sounds to Phoenicia.
     When I see my beak lose its luster,
my Autumn in full bloom,
     I fly to my palm tree where father flew
himself in funeral pyre—
     Watch, as I embalm my ancestor
in our aureate roe,
     for when I rest in fire,
embalm me in my hatchling's embryo.

THE SATIN MYTH

Humbled by flowers who mimic my
feathers, I am not as gentle one look may see.
                              Touch me, I will not break.
          Born from sky, I have no legs, no feet.
You may call me the cloud-ocean merman.
                                   I have nothing on land—
          Face on the rim of sun, I hold your rosy light—
The world's beating flame.

          Wavering pride says I rose from ashes
to claim my royal-colored plumes
          in the body of a lion
                                   head and wings of Eagle.
Invisible I fly, watching king fate
          reel at your past and future,
but no defined paths knot my satin threads.
                              This is why I am Paradise.

BEAK BIRD

Rest with me in the canopy
of viny dreams
as tail and wings cradle
my air-tight beak.

All who live beneath heavy
clouds wonder its creation.
Totems and dances sing
of rainbows who painted my mandible,

I fathered fruited showers
to free me from
the cage of ash
binding you, to you, to me.

Enveloped under flamed Phoenix
feathers, my flesh is shade
which fades the quenchless
passion flowers.

Rouged illusion,
the unsheathed blade,
hides my frailty
so I may bridge rainforest with stars.

Loud is my wreath of chroma,
but not as roaring as my cry
to be entranced by night's lullaby
so I may court the silent boughs.

If you do not eat
my skin
and do not burn
my bones,

I can teach your voice,
your fingers the life of muse
so you may ferry my endless river
to those three dusky lanterns.

ART OF THE DANCE

From thin leaves to papers squared,
through the ritual of folding art,
carefully make one thousand me.
I may grant one wish (maybe two) of silver
chance or longevity.
You may choose your thousand-year gift.

I can admit,
I probably should not have aided
the one killed by thieves
(I am not violence nor vengeance),
but pygmies deserve a death
best served in a crimson arena.

I carry budding flowers
and baby animals by beak
by back I draw the sun close to Earth
when I feel the end of the frost dream,
spring depends on me.

I do not thread through time
for I choose
to whither every thousand
so I may ferry you to the painter's
field, while I boat tiny birds across the Nile.

We mate to search for the icy bloom
and lift her away on our long necks.
Watch us fly in mesh flocks
so we do not drop
her. Our alarming purrs mute virgin screams.

All we know is the craft of moving music
you mimic our courting dance, to celebrate,
to make peace,
but we copy your two-foot stance
and meet at your eyes.

My family, your family,
there is no difference.
Mono-mates are ideal.
Unlike you, we exist in sky,
and land once an autumn.
Earthbound, you cling to the ground.

HEAVEN'S VAULT

Crack the egg filled
with unborn tears
there lives my gaze-
less eyes ablazed
by venom I sip from hissing
flute. My panacea—
snakes of emerald
who crawl
the blue boy's dance floor—
morphs from shadow's
poison to solar-tongued blood.
His mooned lotuses,
lotused hands,
trembled with desire
for this one green-gold feather
to rest upon his crown—
A quill light enough to test
hearts who feared
the belly of bones,
hearts who yearned
for my rebirth.
Those eyes once belonged
to red jealousy,
once belonged
to the warring elephant,
once belonged
to love who sacrificed
eternal life for one's grave bound.
And now, I own the tail
no throne would soon forget,
for each plume homes

the whisper of a star
and one of your prayers.
When I'm disrobed
of those mysteries
then broiled, braised, eaten,
strangers know all your secrets.

THE URN OF NYX

Unaware she had found her fire
blind to the idea her mate was the veil
covering her face and toes,
alone in a bath of frozen wine
she birthed the broods of man's fragility;
Sleep, Death, Pain, Doom.

While we meet our Orions in the shallowed tides
and learn that the hunter desires honey-tongued
Serpens, she arrives on misty chariot
pulled by the shadow of a horse
drawn from the stale lungs of Atlas.

Echo in the hanging gardens of waning
poppies meets with the invisible Elf
Owl whose clever eons coil
through the wrinkles on the weeping
tree. She lives around the raven and the crane
by the Styx, when morning enters.

What is Night, but a crying reflection
of our star-dotted Milky Way?
Like the moon, a mirror of our tender
rays—a light which dwells
on the vulture's beak and courts
our cold fingers home.

There is no shade to nail against the heaven's blue.
There is no noctua to pin on your door.
Scarlet oceans are more
various than the whispering leaves.
Goddess' bottomless, purple fruit is more
intricate than her aureole of darkened rain.

A falling star
is it worse than a falling planet
where no ghosts capture
the rarity of prowling humming birds?

Light, light is our umbra's craze
and all she wants is her mantle of night
to cover the world with her husband's sperm,
but in her consort's seed
lies the slumbering king of dreams.

WINGMAKERS

Walls that empty loose memories
into a playground of the Dog Star
walks with Orion, the hunter,
to feel forbidden feathers.

These are the birds who unearth—
un-sky forgotten fears that trump
gravities only hold onto your fingertips.
Pale orchid moons waffling nightingales

help me dig for stories past,
will gift starry paths to worlds
once unknown. Unhurried
wings understand: waiting is letting

world's lost answers come to you.
You, bird, have nothing to do with
night or gales or nighting or galeing,
but the Wingmaker's song holds a pitcher

filled with daylight's wonder
and if you drink, Orion will court
your tired photographs of the sun episode,
which teeters and totters

on your sand-gummed eyelashes.
These are the common feathers
you may see on the branches
of soiled wood, but they live

in the seraphic forests guarding spoken word—
written only on palms,
planets, and pupils of your ancient,
doubled ladders. They rest

upon shoulders of old cosmogony.
This is your peephole
to the map
of constellations.

POSTLUDES

THE MUSES LEAVE APOLLO

Your father has no eyes;
          you mirror the sun
who punctured fleeting
                    whim
          upon your marbled bones—

you muses hold no eyes as well.
                    Melancholy
is a frozen wreath
'round your fingertips

so tears transform to language
bound by others' silent dreams.

Though the air he breathes,
divine,
          father's crown plucks
          dire paint to gild
the moon of your cold feet.

Gustave Moreau tasked you
                    to light
          the world,
Calliope your herald—
but as I stare
through your moment stilled

your domain burns like
a candle to the sun.

And I realize
          time would have
                    nothing
to hold if you did not
flee the nest.

COLUMBA THE DOVE

For a creature so small, you have withstood the tests of time. While holding an olive branch, you represent peace in the eyes of religion. And even though you battle to bloodshed as younglings, in your prime you are most devoted to loving your mate. You show humanity how to kiss, in your courtship, and how to love in death, for you know no other relationship in your life.

Ancient Greece (Jason and the Golden Fleece)

When we are embraced by your glowing stars, you can be seen as either perched on the stern of the celestial ship or flying from her legends. When Jason sailed his argonauts to retrieve the Golden Fleece, you were sent out of the grand ship in Jason's hands. You flew with faster speed than the swift current that stole his sandal through the never ending clash of the rock Symplegades. Your wings calmed the islands and the Argos sailed unharmed.

Noah's Ark

Similar to the myth of Jason, you were released by the old hands of Noah, but this time to see if the flood had calmed her waves and brought land to the faithful after the flood. You returned with an olive branch in your beak—a sign land was nigh.

DRACO THE DRAGON

Although many stories surround your winding torso Draco, you were pinned against the night for your times in Greece and Rome.

Greco-Roman (The Founder of Thebes and The Titan Wars)

Murdered by Cadmus, this is the most popular story of your arrival in the starry heavens. When Cadmus' sister, Europa, was kidnapped by Jupiter in the costume of Taurus, he was ordered by his father to go find her, never to come back unless Europa was with him.

The hero meandered with purpose around the world, for no mere mortal can take back what Jupiter has stolen, so Cadmus begged Apollo's oracle to tell him what land he should tread.

Cadmus did what Apollo said and found the perfect place for his new city. He sent his attendants to find fresh water to offer as a gift to Jupiter, and they wandered into a cave of springs, where poisoned death lurked in the darkness, for as they were getting water they were all killed by you as war's serpent; a most alluring creature with golden crest; fire in your eyes, body filled with poison. With teeth more menacing than a shark or tiger's, your words burned from trifurcate tongue.

Worried for his companions, Cadmus wearily traveled into the cave and found and killed you easily with his spear. Under Minerva's word, he sowed your thousand teeth, where warriors who battled until five were left, claimed that dirt as the city of Thebes.

***

This was not your first encounter with Minerva though, for when you were Draco the Titan who battled with the Olympians for ten years, she killed and threw you into the night sky, to eternally freeze around the North Pole.

(The Trials of Heracles)

When the queen planted her tree in the sacred groves of Atlas, as Landon, you became the misfortunate guardian of those golden apples; tasked to keep Atlas' nymphs away who guarded the tree from every other being.

Only you know if you had a hundred heads and were the child of the monstrous Typhon and Echidna, but most everyone believes you were the child of Ceto and Phorcys, in which case you only had one head.

As part of his twelve labors of immortality, you were not warned that the half-god Heracles was asked to steal some golden apples from Hera's tree. He killed your one or one hundred heads with his poisoned arrows and easily stole the apples. But the goddess mourned for you as she placed your looped image in the sky amid the constellations.

PEGASUS

Ancient Greece (Origin, Hippocrene, Bellerophon)

Pegasus, with your wings of white, the stallion of light, you were birthed from the neck of the beheaded Medusa when Perseus sought his prize in her. Before snakes became her crown, your mother was once beautiful and young. When Athena caught her being defiled by the sea, the goddess made her face so ugly, anyone who looked upon her turned to stone. And when Perseus killed the gorgon, not only you sprang forth form your mother's blood, but also the warrior Chrysaor; both of you, Poseidon's sons.

***

After your miraculous birth, you first flew to the home of Muses— Mount Helicon—and befriended the storytellers. By striking the ground with your powerful hooves, you created a spring of poets named Hippocrene, for it is said those who drank from the cool waters were blessed with the gift to write poetry.

***

Your wings were once untamable, but when Bellerophon found you, he used a golden bridle given to him by Athena, to calm your wild ego. This hero, who was sent by King Iobates to kill the Chimaera who devastated the king's land, swooped down on the Chimaera and killed the monster with his lance and arrows. After several successful, heroic deeds, Bellerophon grew an ego bigger than yours. You let him try to fly to Olympus and join the gods, knowing he would not succeed. You however, made it to the mount of gods where you were fated to carry Zeus' thunder and lightning. Eventually, you were placed among the constellations with only the top half of your body portrayed.

CYGNUS THE SWAN

Ancient Greece (Cygnus and Orpheus)

Son of oceans, Cygnus, defeated and smothered to the ground by Achilles, you will remain forever, a swan by the fatherly hands of Neptune.

***

Grieving son of music and poetry, most respected musician in Ancient Greece, Orpheus, why did you not see the Thracian woman dance with Dionysus? While you mourned for your dead lover, she staked your heart under his orders. Celebrated and loved by all your listeners, upon death you were placed among the heavens to spend eternity with your harp, Lyra. The noble swan, your choice of creature.

***

And Cygnus son of Sthenele, bringer of the name for these four main stars, you were very close friends with Phaethon (son of Helios or Apollo, the sun deity). Your only friend died in the River, Eridanus, after attempting to drive the sun chariot. Unaware, unable to control his course, Phaethon careened across sky, scorching the heavens and Earth (Gaia). When Gaia pleaded to Zeus to stop the fires, Zeus struck down the sun child with his mighty thunderbolt and severed his tie to this world. Overcome with grief, that sadness transformed you into a swan. You are tethered to water as you abhor fire, dirt, and sky.

CORVUS THE RAVEN

Wiser than the old owl, you, Raven, hold the heaviest burdens and laurels upon your fragile wings, of any creature with beak and feathers.

Greco-Roman (Coronis and The Feast of Zeus)

In a time of peace between you and the sun, when you were his right-hand man, he gave you a noble task of keeping a watchful eye on Apollo's pregnant lover, Coronis. You reported back with the unwelcome news that she was having an affair with a mortal man. Apollo cursed you, and your color changed from its former silver hue to the present black. Corona was killed by Apollo's sister Artemis. The unborn child was rescued and raised as Asclepius, father of medicine.

*****

A thousand years passed, and you became the sun's enemy. When Apollo lived in his earthly form, he wanted to give his father (Zeus) a feast. You were given a simple task; fill the chalice with water, but on your way you noticed a fig tree. Lust for the sweet fruit, fueled with sloth hanging over your shoulders, you rested there until the figs ripened. Gluttony bellowed in your bowels; a sound you could not ignore. Feasting yourself upon them, you finally remembered your prompt errand, and your fear of Apollo's anger was valid. Was it fair to accuse the slithering serpent? The deity of prophecy knows a lie when he sees it. Your excuse that the Hydra had prevented you from filling the cup by blocking the flow of the spring only had him punish you with eternal thirst. At least he was kind enough to alleviate your thirst only when your lover was not ripe. At least he was giving enough to immortalize you next to your cursed cup (Crater) and snake, only for the Hydra to stand as an obelisk and guard the water from the everlastingly thirsty, you, Corvus, so you now sit within sight of water, but never can you drink.

Norse (Odin's Birds of Rumor)

Royalty flowed through your veins as Odin's omniscient pets. For being twin crows, you did not fight as much as Loki and Thor. In your life as Hugin (mind) and Munin (memory), you flew around the world to learn of humanity's news and then returned to Odin every night. You were treated as more than pets; you were gods yourself as you prettily sat on each of Odin's shoulders and murmured to him every worldly rumor. You chose others to hear your whispers as well. Throughout time, many lived their entire lives not being able to hear you. Others listened more carefully and were able to speak with you or eavesdrop on your conversations.

Ukrainian (The Rainbow Feathers)

You do not speak much of your life when you were filled with every color. Ukrainian legend speaks of your beautifully stained feathers and lovely singing voice. You were a sacred Fallen Angel, and when you fell from heaven your plumage turned black and you lost your song. Do you think your former beauty will return if Paradise is restored?

North American Indian (Trickster and Thief of the Sun)

Among the native tribes of the New World you are both creator and trickster. Raven, you must have had brilliant countenance. It is sung in their lore that you and peacock were immortal friends. To free your boredom, you both decided to paint each other. As you painted peacock radiantly, his greed snatched the better of him as he painted you black; keeping the colors for himself. Maybe you just gave your band of chroma to your closest friend? Or maybe black suits you best.

*****

You are the thief of light; stealing the sun from gods then taking it back from humanity. At first the light-giving stars were stuffed in a box by the chief of Heaven—humans lived in darkness. You did not tolerate that for long and planned to steal that precious box. Taking the shape of a leaf, you floated in a stream where the chief's daughter drank you whole, rooting your schemes as an infant boy with raven hair and beady eyes. When she gave birth, you quickly bewitched the chief. And soon after he could not resist your babyness, so you began to cry for the light filled box. Grandfather innocently gave it away. You proceeded to change into your grand bird shape and carried the box through the skies, towards the heavens where the stars would lie. Dropping that fragile box, you made the light brake into tiny fragments, giving rise to the era of stars, the moon, and the sun.

*****

You knew the world, for humans, shouldn't be easy though. Living many lives, Earth without hardships is no life at all, no? You changed the world while insects, magpies, and young-minded beings dreamt a life you did not give. Apart from your creating times, your feathers were believed to have changed the world afterwards to a less comfortable place. You enjoyed watching humans struggle with your world's complexities and strenuous lots. And when you finally befriended humanity, you stole back their sun to watch them freeze in a twelve-hour night.

Aesop Fable ("Necessity—the mother of invention.")

None of this changes how you utilize your time and genius. Your intelligence is unquestionable, and Aesop paid tribute to your ingenuity. When thirst overcame your spirit, Apollo's curse wearing on your wings, you came upon a pitcher filled with enough water to quench your Caw, but not enough to drink. Immediately you noticed your beak was too short to reach the water. If you had tipped the pitcher over, the water would be no more. And then it dawned on you to throw pebbles in the pitcher till the water rose and reached the top.

NOCTUA THE OWL

Owl, with your human-shaped eyes and alluring hoot, you are the bird that captures mystery in the lore of the world. You are most feared, and most loved.

North American Indian (Prophet and Omen)

There are a number of tribal stories about you, Owl. In most, you were the divine prophet. However, when you were the Burrowing Owl, the Hopi tribe held your feathers as sacred, believing you to be a symbol of their god of the dead. As such, you were a guardian of the underworld, and all life that grew in rich dirt.

Ancient Greece (Little Owl)

Athena was once your keeper; the great Greek goddess of wisdom and war. You filled her lonely mind. Impressed with your wisdom, and levels of seriousness, she chose you over the crow, to be her familiar. Little did she know the crow was more clever. You may not like the confines of a name, but Athena called you her Little Owl, *Athene noctua*, for the shape you took inside the Acropolis.

Ancient Rome and After (Nail your Wings to a Door)

Throughout the ancient world, nailing you to the door was considered a way to keep evil at bay. Your wings, cruxed and fastened to the wooded entrance, began in ancient Rome, after you foretold the death of the beloved Julius Caesar. Much like most everything else in Rome, this practice thrived in other areas, including Great Britain up through the eighteenth century, where, if you were nailed to a barn door, livestock would be safe from fire or lightning. Contrary to popular thought at the time, you were also known as a harbinger of ill tidings and doom throughout Europe. Your countenance inspired many writers to make you a symbol of death and destruction.

AQUILA THE EAGLE

While your feathers are stained by blood and water, you are the face for all gods of sky. In your purest form, bird with eyes so yellow, so fierce, you show humanity how to overcome the bull and serpent, yet you give into them yourself, and that is why you are eagle. Let your feathers remain sacred and your talons remain man's highest achievements as you skin-walk your road through history.

Persia (Roc the King Bird of Prey)

Roc was once your most feared mask, but you never ceased to amaze sailors that you saved and travelers alike. Marco Polo wrote of your giant, white feathers you carelessly dropped on mountains and waters. So began the hunt for your eggs and proof of your existence. Old stories spoke of elephants you broke to pieces only to nourish your young. You even took the head of the Solar bird and the serpent Naga, but why can we not find you, a giant, now? They believe you are Phoenix or Thunderbird.

Aztec and Vedic (The Sun God and Garuda)

Your enemy remains the serpent. And in many threads you are seen swallowing snakes. As the Aztec sun god, you transformed into an eagle to show to your people you were real. Your power to swallow poison proved you were a god.

***

When you were the great Garuda, slithering Naga fed your pride and sated your hunger for war.

North American Indian (The Sacred Eagle)

Majesty graces your wings, and to many Indian tribes, you remain sacred to their stories and ceremonies. You created thunder and lightning by beating your wings through the winds and clouds. For the Pawnee, you guarded fertility, for you only nest in the highest places.

Ancient Greece (Periphas, Ganymede, and The Pursuit of Nemesis)

Not very many men know you were once the mortal king Periphas. Your virtuous rule was celebrated like that of a god. Most were convinced you were Zeus in human flesh, so in his rage he would have struck you with a thunderbolt, but Apollo, the god you worshiped most of all, intervened. Zeus listened and instead, transformed your kingliness into an eagle only to set you beside his throne. Your lover, your wife begged to be with you as a bird, so she was changed into a Vulture.

***

Named for your eyes that see all under the sun, you saw Ganymede, the young prince of Troy, out of all the young men of Greece. You stole him for Zeus, who desired him and made him immortal so his youth would be his prison. Ganymede became the cup bearer for

Olympus. You still steal him in the stars as Aquila and Aquarius.

***

You are both the guardian of thunderbolts and the arrows of Eros, but in your curiosity, concerning the latter, you accidentally shot Zeus and made him love-struck.

***

A hunger for power, changed to raw carnality, the god of dark clouds turned to swan to fulfill his selfish lust for the goddess Nemesis, who hid from him in the guise of a goose.

PHOENIX

You belong to everyone everywhere, dear Phoenix, not just Arabia. You are the wandering sacred fire whom lost, lonely wanderers may see in the dark. Your wings trail from Greece to China.

Phoenicia

Phoenicia received her name when you guided the brother of Cadmus from Egyptian Thebes to Syria. As he reigned at Sidon and stole your name, he titled those people Phoenicians and the province Phoenicia to preserve your legacy.

***

Although you are twin to eagle, with radiant scarlet, crimson, gold drapes, and a purple gold tail instead of black or brown, and white, you serve as beacon of goodness and hope, while he stands as pillar of terror and wrath.

Egypt

You are also twin to Benu, the great bird of Egyptian myth, only because your name gives allusions to many different words. You could be your home, the palm tree, the Mauve Heron, or even the morning star. However, it comes as no surprise that you are the most humble of feathered flyers and choose to be the reborn instead.

Ancient Greek

No matter what nature threw at you, you made it a quest to return your egg where land remains immortal. Depending on where the winds told you to go, the temple of Hyperion (titan of light), or the Egyptian sun city, Heliopolis, were your destinations. You sought worthy these places for your hatchling to be raised.

***

Living through 500 years, your gift is to watch the rise and fall of empires, history, time, humanity, just as you flow with their nature. You are their flame of reincarnation; that second chances at life indeed exist. There was a time when amethyst, the sheen of your royal cloak, was hard to find. And to this day, when your cloak loses shine, you wander no longer to your palm tree. You father a funeral pyre with aromatic twigs you have collected in your life. The sun's rays embrace your face, and with a beat of your heart and wings, you harness the fire of the star and combust into your own ashes where a new life awaits your spirit.

APUS THE BIRD OF PARADISE

You have no feet to land on trees or soil. Your family of swifts yearn for your mating dance and stained plumes, for you can change your costume. All the birds of stars, combined in one being, flows in your blood; this is your destiny.

***

Maybe you are paradise on earth, the Garden of Eden heaven. Or perhaps you are angels taking the face of rare beauty. You can be the messenger of whispered wisdom or the king of winds. You hover the airs like human beings tread rock laden roads. When they see or hear your legend feathers, you morph from Eagle to Phoenix. Like the crane, man has tried to mimic your mating dance. Watch, as they raise up the wings they wish to claim, stretch out their necks, and elevate their exquisite plumes, keeping them, like you, in a continual vibration.

***

You fly with face towards the sun until you fly no more. On your shining back the female lays her eggs. Younglings born in the clouds know the snake wind language; know how to weave the breeze through their wings and fly to chase the royal sun home to starry ocean.

TUCANA THE TOUCAN

Your call echoes and booms through the canopies to the ancient forest floor, but this is only one of your distinctive layers. Puzzled science wonders the origins of your banana beak; legend and lore hold all your mysteries.

Aztec

As the messenger of their gods, radiant colors were your gift from the rainbows. The Aztecs worshiped you in their rituals so you would bring rain. They would wear your feathers in a head-like regalia to plead with you for storms. If rain did not come within a few days, you would be sacrificed to the gods on ceremonial pyre.

Inca and Maya

Most sacred to the Incas and treasured like gold by the Maya, your beak stood as a mystic symbol and their tribal totem. The shaman believed you were the incarnation of a god and you bridged the rainforest with the spirit world. Your face, carved onto totems, signified the common roots between you, life, and their ancestry. You carry a jinx in your feathers though, which the ancient Incas and Maya shared to present generations. In your native home, you dance with darker spirits to keep human teeth from devouring your flesh; for if the father of an infant ate your skin and blood, the newborn would fade from his arms, never again to be cradled.

GRUS THE CRANE

Eldest of them all, your timeless feathers have been respected, admired, and even feared throughout centuries and many different cultures.

Asia

In Asian myth and art, you stand as a symbol of the one who has passed the test of time. Forever, you have been the ferry of souls as they ride on your back to the heavens. In Japan they believe you live for thousands of years. Is it true if a person folds one thousand pieces of paper into your shape, they will be granted their greatest wish?

Ancient Greece

In Ancient Greece you brought blackberry winter and avenged Ibycus, the man said to be killed by a band of thieves. Crane, you were the last being he saw circling over his head. Vengeance is unusual to your nature, but you carried out his final wish. One day when the thieves were enjoying a show at the local theater, you began to loom over their heads until one of the them shouted, "behold the avengers of Ibycus." You brought peace and justice to his corrupt spirit as they confessed to the murder.

***

Afterwards you transformed into Apollo, the sun god, to herald spring and light after winter's rage, then hid as crane again to visit your mortal lovers.

***

Like everything in history however, you can not avoid your horrific shortcomings. The art on walls and urns speaks of your war with Pygmies. Instead of finding your own food and breeding grounds you migrated down to their land in the winter and stole their only crops. They battled nobly, tooth and blood, every season to save their crops and their lives. You do not feel regret for the soul you did not put properly to rest.

African Lore

Some people are convinced that you are aware of your own gifts though; that you possess self-knowledge. So, Crane, you must be aware of the pain you have caused. That doesn't seem to change the god-like view humans have of you.

Egypt

When Europe went to Egypt they saw your warmth and kindness. You only migrated to Egypt to pick up yellow wagtails and other small birds on your back and carry them across the Nile.

Inuit

You are even revered in some of the coldest places in the world. Did you find your beautiful Inuit girl? She stood alone in her village, waiting for you it seemed. Her loneliness was unbearable for you to see and not do anything. You had to pick her up and carry her away on your large wings. She was really that beautiful when you saw her? Love at first glance? As other cranes flew in a dense flock below, prepared to catch her if she fell, you cried your loudest cry to mute her bloody screams.

***

Humans will remain amazed by your nature. You are the most human of all the birds as you stand, two-footed, the same height as the thinking, naked, monkeys. You share the same lifespan and similar social structures.

***

With all the history you are known for, your dancing is most famous. Everyone has been trying to recreate the crane dance for years. How is it that you move the way you do? Each art is remarkably unique as you all have some form of this peace-keeping, mating dance. They mimic because they want to reside in the stars with you.

PAVO THE PEACOCK

With a cape of blue eyes to see greater knowledge, you have watched how your beauty remains a divine message through the ages. As humanity is awe stricken by your fanning feathers, when your plumes become the crown of gods, they know to find truth in the music of their heart.

Yazidi (The Peacock Angel)

When the ancient Tigris and Euphrates rivers cradled thriving man, you were their center; their emanation of divinity. They named you Melek Taus, the light of god, for you were the most benevolent angel to redeem your throne. Although you did not roam those lands in your avian form, they named you the peacock angel, for you created the cosmos from an all-auric egg, like the blue-green iridescence of your trailing ornament. You knew yourself and bowed to no one. You wept for seven thousand years, filled seven jars of tears to quench hell's fire. You did not rule the fires, nor let the fires rule you, for you are incapable of impurity.

Hinduism (Krishna and Murugan)

In ancient India, you who swallow snakes to charge your quills with light, were close to the blue-colored god, Krishna. With his flute and heavens on his back, he danced upon Kaliya's hundred and ten hissing heads, to kill the poisonous Naga. Krishna's music enchanted the king of peacocks who gave the young god a feather to live on his crown.

***

Once the chariot for the Hindu God of war, Murugan (brother of Ganesha with the head of an elephant), who rode you into war with human illness, pain, and fear. You were his weapon as the destroyer of serpents, the face of ego.

Ancient Egypt (Feather of Balance)

Maat, the winged balance of order for the deceased's heart, required only one of your pinions to weigh against the soul. Judgement took place in the Hall of Two Truths. A day and age where balance in life was goodness, the unharmonious heart was fed to the crocodile-headed goddess, Ammit, never to reach paradise.

Buddhism (Guanyin the Compassionate)

In the days and nights you listened to the crying world, Guanyin became your mask and name. Love and compassion filled your five-colored song, for when you were granted immortality, you chose to remain amongst the mortals to aid in their seeking truth.

Babylon and Persia (Guardian of Kings)

Among the royals in the ancient city of Babylon and cities of Persia, your face and feathers are seen in engravings upon their thrones. As their guardian, you gifted them with blazing fortune.

Greco-Roman (Argus)

Your plumage was given to you from the jealous goddess, Hera (Juno). Those 200 eyes, plucked from the head of Argus, kept Zeus away from his pure, white cow—Io. Sun-sinoued eyes rest in your tail, to preserve the short life of Argus.

Christianity (All-seeing and Rebirth)

Those eyes became the symbol for the omniscient god and church. As a mirror of Phoenix, you also represented resurrection, renewal, and immortality, for you gained new and more beautiful feathers every year. You guard divine secrets as heaven's vault.

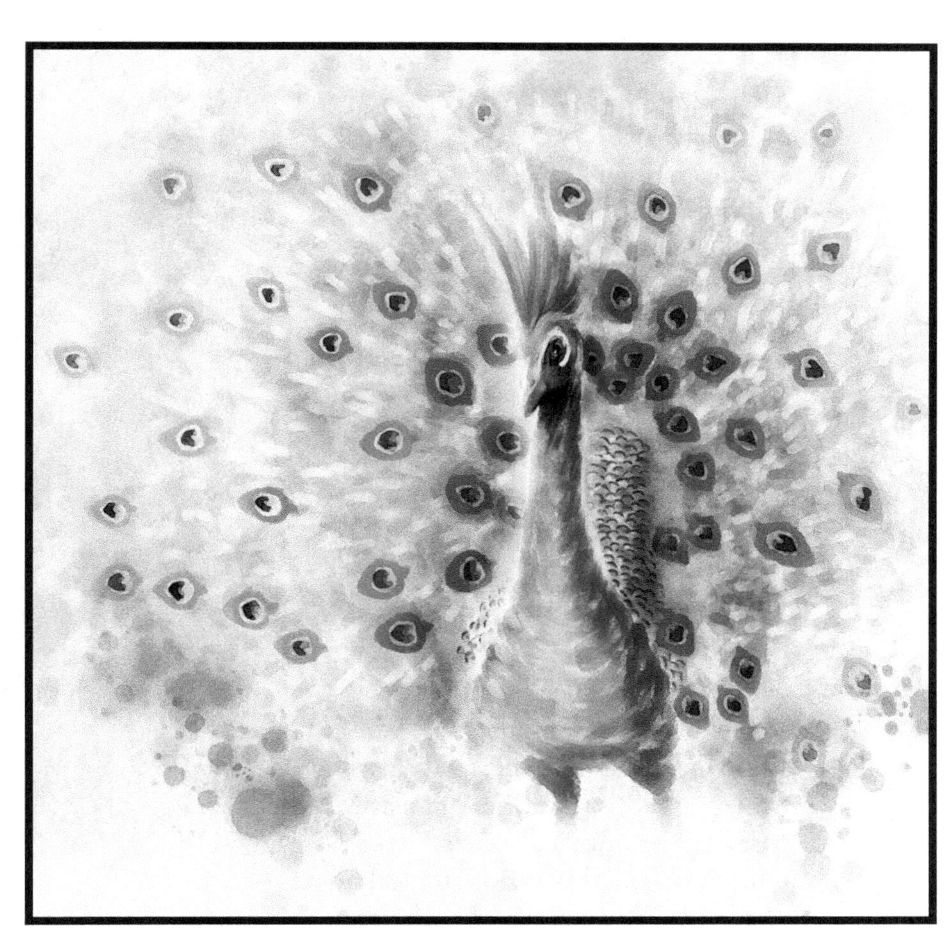

NO LIGHT STEALS MY MEMORY

After King Beryl
of the sky
and blazing sun
lay to rest, my nightly
ritual begins with my luminescent
decanter as I pour a glass
of nature's ruby panacea.
The first sip among her dark wings
is always the comfort I yearn,
but after the fourth, fifth, sixth,
until my jar is empty,
her blood fills my body
with a warm, tame flame.

The day's shackles
who bind my mind,
who bind the serpents tale
of fire, break from mother's
strong hand—Night fills my veins
while stars whisper stories of great heroes
past and her muzzled secrets.
During these lightless hours, I feel home—
The breeze, the darkness who holds
every color, the twinkling children of void,
Earth's sanguine fluid,
all welcome me like the orchid
welcoming mourning cloak

Naked on my window sill,
spilling all my dreams upon
her son's tongue,
I dive into Night's arms, infinitely pale.
She catches me,
picks me up and places my puppet
among the poets, glowing.

Now, at long last,
I sleep.